BUILT FOR SUCCESS

THE STORY OF

Southwest Airlines

Published by Creative Education and Creative Paperbacks
P.O. Box 227, Mankato, Minnesota 56002
Creative Education and Creative Paperbacks
are imprints of The Creative Company
www.thecreativecompany.us

DESIGN BY **ZENO DESIGN**
PRODUCTION BY **TRAVIS GREEN**
ART DIRECTION BY **RITA MARSHALL**
Printed in Malaysia

PHOTOGRAPHS BY Alamy (digitallife, David Osborn, PF-[sdasm2]), Corbis (Michael Ainsworth/Dallas Morning News, Bettmann, Frank Duenzl/dpa, J A Giordano/CORBIS SABA, Daniel Grill/Tetra Images, George Hall, ERIK S. LESSER/epa, Louie Psihoyos, Carl & Ann Purcell, Josef P. Willems, David Woo), Getty Images (Bloomberg, Photoshot, Joe Raedle, Justin Sullivan), Newscom (Nadia Borowski Scott/ZUMA Press, Glen Stubbe/ZUMA Press), SuperStock (Bill Cobb/Bill Cobb)

LIBRARY OF CONGRESS CATALOGING-IN-PUBLICATION DATA
Murray, Laura K.
The story of Southwest Airlines / Laura K. Murray.
p. cm. — (Built for success)
Summary: A look at the origins, leaders, growth, and innovations of Southwest Airlines, the low-fare airline that was founded in Texas in 1967 and today carries more than 100 million passengers annually.
Includes bibliographical references and index.
ISBN 978-1-60818-559-7 (hardcover)
ISBN 978-1-62832-160-9 (pbk)
1. Southwest Airlines Co.—Juvenile literature. 2. Airlines—United States—History—Juvenile literature. I. Title.

HE9803.S68M866 2015
387.76'573—dc23 2014028002

CCSS: RI.5.1, 2, 3, 8; RH.6-8.4, 5, 6, 8

First Edition HC 9 8 7 6 5 4 3 2 1
First Edition PBK 9 8 7 6 5 4 3 2 1

CREATIVE EDUCATION • CREATIVE PAPERBACKS

BUILT FOR SUCCESS

THE STORY OF

Southwest Airlines

LAURA K. MURRAY

SOUTHWEST
SOUTHWEST
SOUTHWEST

On June 18, 1971, at 7:00 A.M., a Boeing 737 jet bearing the words "Southwest Airlines" on its tail departed from Love Field in Dallas, Texas, bound for San Antonio. Piloted by captain Emilio Salazar, the plane was staffed by friendly flight attendants dressed in shorts and go-go boots. The plane coasted down the runway without fanfare. As it lifted off, Southwest cofounder Herb Kelleher and his executives breathed sighs of relief. Their discount airline with low-fare specials was finally up and running. By focusing on energetic employees and flight strategies that saved time and money, Southwest's maiden flight represented a new age in the airline industry. But the little company would need incredible determination to *really* take off—and eventually become one of the most successful airlines in history.

CHAPTER ONE

Getting Off the Ground

One day in 1966, San Antonio businessman Rollin King was deep in conversation with his banker, John Parker. Parker complained that traveling to Texas's major cities was too inconvenient and expensive. What Texas needed, he said, was an airline that would fly within the state.

King, who owned a small air service, agreed—and knew just the person to see. He pitched his plan for a low-fare, intrastate airline to Herb Kelleher, an outspoken local lawyer with experience in the airline industry. The two mapped out a simple route that would connect the cities of the "Texas Triangle": San Antonio in the west, Dallas in the north, and Houston in the east.

On March 15, 1967, their venture became Air Southwest Co. Kelleher based the business model on California's successful Pacific Southwest Airlines (PSA), founded in 1949. After Kelleher, King, and other **investors** raised $543,000 to finance the project, the Texas Aeronautics Commission (TAC) gave Air Southwest approval to fly in February 1968.

Other airlines weren't about to welcome a new competitor into Texas, though. Three of them—Braniff, Texas International (then known as Trans-Texas), and Continental—took out a temporary restraining order that stopped the TAC from

Known for its flight attendants' short and colorful uniforms, PSA operated until 1988.

issuing Air Southwest its certificate to fly. The case went before a Texas district court a few months later. Tensions ran high during the trial that put Air Southwest in the spotlight. The bigger airlines claimed the Texas market had all the carriers, or airlines, it could handle. They said that another airline would burden the state's **economy** with extra air services. When the court ruled against Air Southwest—and an appeals court upheld the decision—the future of the would-be airline seemed doomed.

In 1969, King and other members of the Air Southwest **board of directors** debated whether to shut down. The new business hadn't even had an opportunity to make a **profit**, and it couldn't afford another costly legal fight. Never one to back down from a challenge, Kelleher encouraged the board to "go one more round" with the competitors. He volunteered to represent Air Southwest and pay all the court fees until the company earned money. The board eventually agreed. When Kelleher filed an appeal with the Texas Supreme Court, that court affirmed Air Southwest's right to fly. Not ready to accept defeat, the larger airlines appealed to the United States Supreme Court. On December 7, 1970, the federal court refused to even hear the case—and Air Southwest knew it was in business.

Air Southwest's scrappy founders needed to entrust the fledgling company to someone capable of beginning operations in **debt**, with just $142 in the bank. On January 1, 1971, 50-year-old M. (Marion) Lamar Muse, an airline industry veteran, became Air Southwest's president. After convincing investors to sink their money into the company, Muse focused on the most crucial part of an aviation business: airplanes. He struck a deal with airplane manufacturer Boeing for three new 737-200s. By March, Muse had hired an all-star management team to carry out duties in **marketing**, ground operations, maintenance and engineering, and flight procedures. With decades of experience among them, the "Over-the-Hill Gang" didn't waste time in implementing innovative business practices, many of which remain in use today.

By the 1970s, Braniff owned more than 70 jets and offered flights to Central and South America.

But delays—and legal fees—continued to pile up. At this time, the interstate airline industry was **regulated** by the federal Civil Aeronautics Board (CAB). The CAB controlled fare prices, routes, and schedules. Sometimes, it took the CAB years to approve a new airline. Although Air Southwest planned to fly only within the state of Texas, Braniff and Texas International filed complaints with the CAB. They claimed that Air Southwest might break the rules and try to fly to other states.

On March 29, 1971, the enterprise changed its named to Southwest Airlines Co. By summer, the CAB had thrown out the competitors' complaints, and Southwest appeared ready for takeoff. After Kelleher blocked a last-minute attempt by Braniff to halt operations, he overheard concerns that the local sheriff might try to stop the inaugural flight. A fed-up Kelleher told Muse, "Leave tire tracks on his shirt. We're going, come hell or high water." Finally, four years after its founding, Southwest Airlines began service on June 18. It made 6 round trips from its Dallas headquarters to San Antonio and 12 round trips from Dallas to Houston, charging $20 for one-way fares. By the end of the year, Southwest's 195 employees had helped the airline make more than 6,000 trips, but the young company was suffering financially.

Rather than cut employees, Muse sold a recently purchased fourth plane. Southwest decided to continue with its busy flight schedule meant for four planes with just three. It seemed impossible, but ground operations executive Bill Franklin came up with a solution he called the 10-Minute Turn. "Turning" a plane consisted of all the activities—including unloading, maintenance, cleaning, refueling, and re-boarding—that needed to be done between a plane's arrival at a terminal and its next departure. Franklin threatened to fire whoever couldn't get it all done at the unheard-of pace of 10 minutes. Southwest employees drew comparisons to racetrack pit crews as they sprinted across **tarmacs** for planes upon arrival. The 10-Minute Turn became key to Southwest's very survival. It also gained the airline a reputation for timeliness. Southwest, however, was quickly becoming a household name for something other than its efficient scheduling.

Herb Kelleher described Southwest's business model as an upside-down pyramid with employees on top.

752
SOUTHWE

RUNNING THE SKIES

Known as "the master of gimmick," M. Lamar Muse had a unique marketing approach and keen business sense that were largely responsible for Southwest's early success. And he was willing to go to unusual measures to ensure that success. "We actually bought fuel for a couple of months using Lamar's personal credit card," remembered executive Sherry Phelps. Muse's many accomplishments included his pricing structure that offered discounted tickets for flights at less popular, or "off-peak," times. As a result, more seats were filled, and flights became more profitable. Muse left the company in 1978 after a dispute with the board. He began helping his son, also a former Southwest employee, run a rival airline known as Muse Air. In 1985, Southwest bought Muse Air and renamed it TranStar Airlines. Even after that airline ceased operations in 1987, Muse still called Herb Kelleher "the best friend anyone ever had and the toughest competitor on Earth." Muse died in 2007, widely regarded as an industry pioneer.

CHAPTER TWO

A Class of Its Own

After establishing its position in the airline industry, Southwest focused on the next step to success: making a profit. It had to set itself apart from the more recognizable companies and get people talking.

Discount prices wouldn't be enough to cause a stir, though Southwest's flights of the 1970s were as much as 50 percent less than competing airlines'. "You can have a low-cost carrier, and people still don't fly it because they don't know about it," explained Kelleher. His experienced executives had a plan, and it involved being as outrageous as possible.

When Southwest put out a call for its first flight attendants, the only people invited to apply were attractive, bubbly women. For their interviews, finalists were required to wear a popular type of tight shorts called hot pants. The interviewing panel even included the woman who had trained flight attendants aboard Hugh Hefner's Playboy jet. Southwest's "hostesses" became known for their outfits of orange hot pants and white vinyl go-go boots. The hiring requirements, which some outside observers viewed as **sexist**, would be challenged in the coming years. According to Kelleher, "the [act] kind of fit in with getting known."

Flight attendants weren't the only ones who faced an unusual and competitive

Unlike today's practical styles, flight attendant uniforms of the '70s were designed to be fashionable.

selection process. Pilots were often asked to change into Bermuda shorts to show that they were good sports. Crew members were also handpicked for their outgoing personalities or special "sparkle." Borrowing an idea from PSA, Kelleher used the phrase "Long legs, short nights" to promote the flights and their out-of-the-ordinary cabin crews. Employees were encouraged to sing, dance, and crack jokes with passengers. As researchers Kevin and Jackie Freiberg observed about Southwest employees, "They were nutty, flashy, and very hip when the competition was conventional, businesslike, and very bland."

Southwest, operating out of Love Field just minutes from downtown Dallas, built its entire **brand** around the good-time concept of "love." Under the company **slogan** "Somebody else up there loves you," planes were nicknamed "love birds," cocktails became "love potions," and peanuts "love bites." The airline's passengers, mostly business travelers, rode "Pleasure Class." At least one thing was certain: people could expect something entirely different when they boarded a Southwest flight. "To make up for the advertising we couldn't afford, we decided we were going to be fun, zesty, and a little irreverent to generate a buzz," said Colleen Barrett, Kelleher's legal secretary at the time. Southwest's competitors had certainly taken notice.

In 1973, Southwest offered a half-off sale that charged $13 for all flights to San Antonio. One month later, Braniff advertised the same price on its flights from Dallas to Houston—the only profitable route Southwest had. The move set off a widely publicized battle known as the $13 Fare War. Muse had Southwest place a carefully crafted ad of its own in local Texas newspapers. Headlined "Nobody's going to shoot Southwest Airlines out of the sky for a lousy $13," the ad announced an unusual offer: customers could choose to pay $13, or they could purchase the full $26-fare and receive a free bottle of liquor. The majority of passengers (especially those charging tickets to their company accounts) chose the full-price option. By the end of 1973, Southwest had made its first annual profit and would never suffer a yearly loss again.

Love Field was named for First Lieutenant Moss Lee Love, who died in a 1913 plane crash.

Southwest scored another victory in 1975 when Braniff and Texas International were charged with trying to put the newcomer airline out of business and were fined $100,000. Company leaders traded barbs in the press. Muse especially relished that the larger airlines' tactics had backfired. "If [Braniff] had just let us alone from the very beginning, we'd probably have gone under by now," he commented. Being targeted by Braniff had earned Southwest public sympathy—and made the small airline fight even harder to come out on top.

Southwest had come to see itself as an underdog, and its fighting days weren't over. In the early '70s, its very home came under attack. The trouble had begun in the late '60s (before Southwest's creation), when the CAB ordered all airlines serving Love Field to move to the Dallas/Fort Worth Regional Airport (DFW) once it opened in 1974. Southwest knew its business would suffer if passengers had to travel the extra 20 minutes from downtown Dallas to DFW. Despite challenges filed by the cities of Fort Worth and Dallas, plus DFW, the U.S. Supreme Court upheld Southwest's use of Love Field.

In 1978, president Jimmy Carter signed the Airline Deregulation Act, which freed the airline industry from many aspects of government control. Brand-new airlines could enter the industry and offer competitive prices without fear of legal trouble. In addition, Southwest could offer interstate flights. After receiving CAB authorization for a Houston–New Orleans route in 1979, Southwest set its sights on adding more interstate flights.

The Love Field challengers, however, wanted to ensure Southwest didn't take away their out-of-state business. They pressured Congress to issue a compromise known as the Wright Amendment. The change to the 1979 International Air Transportation Competition Act limited the states to which Southwest could fly nonstop from Love Field (Louisiana, New Mexico, Oklahoma, and Arkansas). It also curbed the number of seats on those flights (no more than 56). Despite the restrictions, Southwest grew rapidly over the next few years, adding aircraft, flights, and passengers.

> *"The warrior mentality, the very fight to survive, is truly what created our culture."*
>
> COLLEEN BARRETT, FORMER SOUTHWEST PRESIDENT

President Carter remarked that the Airline Deregulation Act was "a major step forward for consumers."

Herb Kelleher

EMPLOYEE LOVE

Southwest executives were known for fostering a work environment in which employees felt appreciated and—true to the Southwest mission—loved. In return, employees were fiercely loyal, paving the way for the airline's rise to greatness. "We treated our job like it was our own business," explained one worker. And for some, it *was* their business. In the early 1970s, the airline created the industry's first profit-sharing plan, making 10 percent of the company employee-owned. Each of the original Southwest employees (including flight attendants) became a millionaire, thanks to his or her ownership of company **stock**. "Southwest rewards people who believe in working and playing hard," said cofounder Herb Kelleher. By 2014, 83 percent of Southwest employees were part of a **union**. But early that year, union workers picketed proposed changes to their contracts. "Ever since Herb ... [retired], this has been more of a corporation and less of a family," said union representative Randy Barnes.

CHAPTER THREE

Spreading the LUV

By the 1980s, it seemed that all those early years spent scrambling for survival had paid off. Southwest's executives were confident, the employees loyal, and the service top-notch. The company, operating in the stock market under the symbol "LUV," had good news for its **shareholders**: profits were up and getting bigger.

In 1981, Southwest president and chief executive officer (CEO) Howard D. Putnam resigned after just three years to become president of struggling rival Braniff. (Braniff stopped service in 1982, and several attempts to revive it would fail within a few years.)

At the request of the board, Kelleher soon took over Putnam's positions. Kelleher's priority continued to be expansion throughout the country. By 1983, Southwest was operating out of cities such as Las Vegas, Kansas City, Phoenix, and Los Angeles. That year, the airline carried more than 9.5 million passengers and earned a net income of $40.9 million.

The growing operation depended on skilled employees who were willing to work as a team. Southwest's plane turnarounds, while not always as short as 10 minutes, were still the fastest in the industry. Male flight attendants could now

In the 1980s, Las Vegas experienced a population boom, nearly doubling its inhabitants by 1995.

be seen aboard Southwest flights, thanks to a 1981 lawsuit that challenged Southwest's refusal to hire men for the positions. In 1983, Southwest employed 3,462 people. That number would nearly double within the next five years, as people *wanted* to work for Southwest. It had molded a corporate culture unlike any other. Kelleher, known for his booming laugh and the ever-present cigarette dangling from his mouth, encouraged employees to be themselves and valued them for it. Although the flight attendant uniforms had been toned down, the company often held costume contests and themed flights. Even so, employees were held to high standards in an increasingly cutthroat industry. Barrett, who by then had joined Southwest as corporate secretary, admitted that executives were "drill sergeants" about timeliness. If Kelleher himself ran late for a flight, the plane left without him. The CEO wouldn't have it any other way.

Southwest streamlined its operations as well, striving to make them as efficient as possible. This efficiency began with flying just one type of aircraft, the 737, which allowed employees to become experts. Southwest also focused on direct, "point-to-point" flights rather than flying passengers to a central "hub" city where they changed planes for their final destination. "That [hub-and-spoke system] can lead to a lot of ground time, and we only make money off our planes when they're in the air," explained vice president of ground operations Chris Wahlenmaier in 2012.

As Southwest opened gates in midwestern cities such as St. Louis and Chicago, it appealed to new customers with its discount fares as well as a frequent flier program that earned short-distance travelers free round-trip tickets. In response to a new crop of competitors billing themselves as "low-fare," the airline ran print ads such as "Southwest and other airlines have a love/hate relationship. They hate the way we've lowered airfares, but they'd love to have you think it was their idea." It began operating under the slogan "Southwest: *The* low-fare airline."

With its employee-centric business model, executives figured that if their employees were happy, they would make customers happy enough to return

Southwest executives embraced the opportunity to don elaborate costumes for the annual Halloween party.

again and again—and that would result in happy shareholders. "You put your employees first, and if you take care of them, then they will take good care of you," Kelleher said. He was right. By the late '80s, Southwest had gained a loyal customer base that included many senior citizens, who especially appreciated the affordability and friendliness of the airline. Southwest earned national awards for its "Home for the Holidays" program that enabled thousands of seniors to visit relatives and friends for free. Southwest also turned its attention to other goodwill efforts by naming Ronald McDonald House its primary charity. To raise money for the charity, Southwest began hosting a LUV Classic golf tournament each year.

Southwest was accustomed to media attention after its highly publicized David-and-Goliath beginnings. Now it wanted the spotlight on its own terms. The airline launched new travel deals by teaming up with well-known companies such as Burger King and spokespeople such as professional baseball player Nolan Ryan. It also partnered with SeaWorld of Texas to promote state tourism. After having a 737-300 painted black-and-white to look like a killer whale, Kelleher and Texas mayors kicked off a tour of Southwest destination cities aboard *Shamu One*. The antics didn't stop there. When 1988 laws prohibited smoking on certain flights, Southwest crew members handed out lollipops to "ease" smokers into abiding by the new rules. Passengers loved it.

By the end of the decade, Southwest had become the top airline in California. The Department of Transportation (DOT) rated Southwest as having the best monthly on-time performance and the least lost baggage and complaints of any airline. The award was the first in a long string of monthly "Triple Crowns" for Southwest. In 1989, with record **revenues** exceeding $1 billion, Southwest was named an official "major carrier" by the DOT. But the airline wasn't done growing, and it looked to carve out an even bigger place for itself in the industry.

…back on all my years at Southwest— … the fare wars, the political … t think to myself, 'That was … a lot … wouldn't change a thing."

… KELLEHER, SOUTHWEST COFOUNDER

In 2014, Southwest and SeaWorld ended their long partnership amid animal rights protests.

MSP Welco
Southwest Airli
msp
SOUTHWEST.COM

T. J. LUV

Southwest's notorious battles with Braniff Airlines left a lasting impression on the airline. They also provided the company with a mascot. The character, a little airplane named T. J. LUV, was introduced in an unlikely place—a children's book. *Gumwrappers and Goggles,* by Winifred Barnum Newman, tells the story of a jet named T. J. LUV who battles two bigger planes for the opportunity to fly. A character known only as "The Lawyer" helps T. J. win his court case. The book ends with T. J. speaking to a judge about his dream: "*I want to continue to carry business people to and from the big cities,*" he says. "*I want to give them good service, make their flights smooth, and love, your Honor, I want to give love!*" Southwest soon adopted the plucky red-and-orange jet as its mascot. Newman's book even inspired an early 1980s musical called *Show Your Spirit.*

CHAPTER FOUR

A First-Class Airline

As Southwest entered its 20th-anniversary year, it faced a new type of challenge: rising fuel prices. After the Middle Eastern country of Iraq invaded its oil-producing neighbor Kuwait in 1990, oil prices spiked, and the entire world felt the effects of the Gulf War.

Southwest's employees once again answered the call to ensure Southwest's success. Through a program called Fuel from the Heart, thousands of employees contributed portions of their paychecks to help with fuel costs. Employees also started a program that involved sending letters called "luvgrams" to U.S. troops serving in Operation Desert Storm.

The Gulf War had worsened the economic **recession** already taking its toll on the airline industry. In response to a drop in demand, carriers tried to attract passengers with deep discounts. Lower prices meant less revenue, but Southwest was still seeing profits and performing with its signature flair. As one journalist wrote, "... the company hasn't lost a penny. In an industry plagued by fare wars, recessions, oil crises, and other disasters, this is an astounding feat."

In 1991, the industry publication *Air Transport World* named Southwest "Airline of the Year." Soon after, the DOT reported Southwest was the nation's top airline

Approximately 763,000 U.S. troops served in the Gulf War, which lasted for 6 months.

in customer satisfaction. Customers seemed to respond to Southwest's efforts at taking the stress out of air travel. One of the most popular aspects of that service was Southwest's general seating system. The absence of classes and assigned seats made the boarding process smoother. Flight crews still worked hard to entertain passengers, too. "Good morning, ladies and gentlemen," one flight attendant announced over the intercom. "Those of you who wish to smoke ... please file out to our lounge on the wing, where you can enjoy our feature film, *Gone with the Wind*."

The airline's new corporate headquarters, located in a 254,000-square-foot (23,597 sq m) building at Love Field, was flooded with calls from companies, consultants, and reporters asking for its business secrets. But as Libby Sartain, vice president of people (human resources), later explained, the "secret" was simplicity. And the unique culture wasn't planned—it had come about naturally. "We have literally changed the airline industry and the public's traveling habits and expectations by giving everyone the freedom to fly," she said. "We provide this freedom by offering low fares, frequent flights, and a casual, everyday atmosphere."

Southwest also offered memorable stunts. When it began using the slogan "Just Plane Smart" in 1991, Southwest hadn't realized that a South Carolina company called Stevens Aviation had already coined it. Stevens CEO Kurt Herwald proposed the companies settle the matter out of court—through an arm-wrestling match. Kelleher promptly accepted. Billed as the "Malice in Dallas," the much-anticipated matchup between Kelleher and Herwald attracted major media attention. Hundreds of Southwest employees were given the morning off from work to cheer on their 61-year-old leader. As Kelleher entered the Dallas arena's boxing ring to the *Rocky* theme song, rowdy chants of "Herb! Herb! Herb!" rang out. Though the younger Herwald came out the winner, he let Southwest keep the slogan. The two companies pledged to donate a total of $15,000 to charity as a sign of goodwill.

Morris Air cofounder June Morris based her discount airline on Southwest, using solely Boeing 737s.

But Southwest was doing more than having fun—it was making history. Soon after breaking a DOT record with a 94 percent on-time performance rate, Southwest earned the first-ever annual Triple Crown in 1992. Throughout the '90s, the airline topped business rankings, including *Fortune* magazine's list of "100 Best Companies to Work for in America." In 1993, Southwest bought fellow discount airline Morris Air in a move known as a stock swap. The deal added more than a dozen cities to Southwest's schedule, allowing the airline to expand farther into the Pacific Northwest. As the *New York Times* noted, "The purchase offered additional proof that Southwest is rapidly becoming more [of] a national force than its name suggests." The following year, Southwest saw its first-**quarter** net income rise to $41.8 million.

Southwest was expanding its virtual presence as well. In 1995, Southwest became the first airline with a website when it launched IFlySWA.com. It also experimented with innovative ways for travel agents to book flights through computerized reservation systems.

Although Kelleher had a reputation for zany antics, there was no doubt he had the company's best interests at heart. When Kelleher negotiated with the company's union, the Southwest Airline Pilots' Association (SWAPA), to take a five-year pay freeze starting in 1995, he voluntarily applied the freeze to himself. "We're not afraid to show our people that we're not in it for ourselves," he said. One *Fortune* article asked, "Is Herb Kelleher America's best CEO?" Another stated, "Kelleher's most remarkable story of all, without a doubt, is how he built Southwest Airlines ... into the most successful airline in history."

But Southwest, by then the fourth-largest carrier in the U.S., was on the brink of major changes in 2001. Kelleher decided it was time to step down in May but remained chairman of the board. Barrett took over operations as Southwest president, while Jim Parker became CEO. The airline also introduced the color blue to its signature orange-and-red plane exteriors. Months later, an unforeseen tragedy would change the airline industry—and the world—forever.

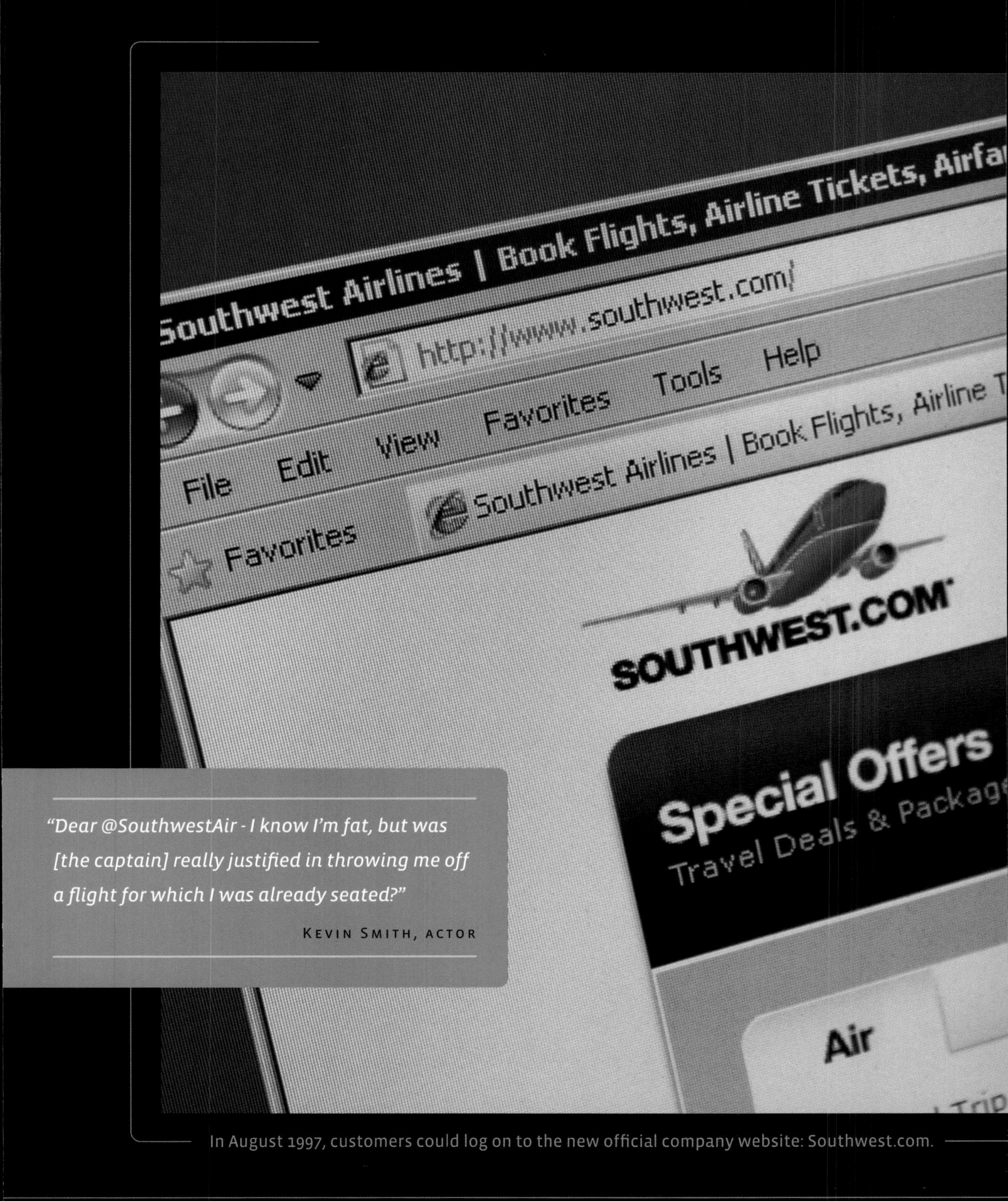

"Dear @SouthwestAir - I know I'm fat, but was [the captain] really justified in throwing me off a flight for which I was already seated?"

KEVIN SMITH, ACTOR

In August 1997, customers could log on to the new official company website: Southwest.com.

www.hewittusa.com
MESA CA US

BETTING ON FUEL

Southwest's financial success can be attributed, in part, to its approach to skyrocketing fuel prices. In a process called fuel hedging, companies can sign a contract for how much they will pay for fuel at a later date. This is a gamble, because the company must pay the agreed price, no matter what. Led by a team that included then executive vice president customers Colleen Barrett and chief financial officer (CFO) Gary Kelly, Southwest committed to fuel hedging in 1999 and locked in how much it would pay. As fuel prices spiked in 2001, Southwest's strategy worked. The airline paid much less than competitors did throughout the 2000s. But by 2012, the hedging strategies had become less effective, and the airline looked to make up the savings in other ways. "The big game changer the last decade has been fuel costs," Kelly said. "Our costs are substantially higher today if for no reason than that."

CHAPTER FIVE

A Post–9/11 World

September 14, 2001, was a somber day as Southwest's airplanes resumed service from Love Field. Three days before, terrorists had hijacked four American Airlines and United Airlines passenger jets in New York, Washington, D.C., and Pennsylvania, resulting in the deaths of nearly 3,000 people.

A new era of air travel began, as more restrictions and costly security measures were put in place in an effort to avoid future catastrophe. Business writer Eric Goldschein points out that in all of airline history, "... the years following the 9/11 attacks proved to be the most tumultuous and formative." Southwest—like all airlines—had to adapt quickly to remain successful in a world forever scarred by such a disastrous air-travel security breach.

Kelleher once explained that a Southwest philosophy was to "manage in good times so you're ready for bad times." Several airlines filed for **bankruptcy** soon after 9/11, as many distrustful potential passengers decided against flying. Over the next few years, the airline industry laid off thousands of employees and lost billions—except Southwest, which avoided layoffs and was the only major U.S.

airline to post a profit each year. By 2003, Southwest was officially the largest low-fare carrier in the U.S. It transported the most monthly passengers of any **domestic** airline.

Some of Southwest's nonstop flights, however, were still limited by the Wright Amendment (although Alabama, Kansas, Mississippi, and Missouri had since been added to Southwest's allowable destinations under Wright). Gary Kelly, Southwest's CEO since 2004, began calling for lawmakers to "set LUV free." Finally, a compromise known as the Wright Amendment Reform Act of 2006 was signed by president George W. Bush. The deal allowed Southwest to operate domestic nonstop flights out of Love Field. In exchange, Love Field would be remodeled and its gates reduced from 32 to 20. Southwest would control 16 gates, while other airlines would control the remaining 4. But because some changes would not go into effect until late 2014, Southwest's executives looked for other solutions in the meantime. Southwest partnered with fellow airlines in a common practice known as code-sharing to operate "shared" flights. This allowed Southwest to gain entry into more cities around the country.

Unfortunately for the airline industry, the economic recession of the late 2000s hit hard. The number of passengers declined, and industry revenue fell off dramatically. One way Southwest avoided layoffs was by allowing employees to retire early. Still, shareholders worried the airline would see its first losses. Just after Barrett retired and Kelleher stepped down as board chairman in 2008, Kelly eased concerns by announcing, "With the weak domestic economy and unprecedented jet fuel prices, we are pleased to report our 69th consecutive quarter of profitability."

During the recession, Southwest once again set itself apart from the competition in a big way. Besides letting passengers change their flights for free, Southwest became the only major airline that did not charge for checked luggage, even though the extra fees would have raked in millions. (However, Southwest did charge for other services, such as early check-ins.) Customers

Kelleher rallied with employees for an end to the Wright Amendment, calling the restrictions "goofiness."

appreciated the "Bags Fly Free" approach and free flight-change policy—as well as Southwest's refusal to cut its staple in-flight snack: peanuts.

In 2011, Southwest bought Florida-based AirTran Airways. The move expanded Southwest's cities once again and helped bring the company's 2012 total operating revenue to $17.1 billion. But Southwest struggled to keep pace with the rapid growth rate of years past. As the largest low-fare airline in the U.S., it felt pressure from other airlines such as Delta as well as low-fare rivals such as JetBlue and Spirit. High fuel prices prompted leaders to announce in late 2013 that Southwest would pull out of several smaller cities to focus on larger markets. Meanwhile, Southwest lost more bags per passenger in 2013 than any other airline. It was flying more passengers to more cities than ever before—but serving larger, busier airports meant more delays. The *Wall Street Journal* reported that Southwest had "begun to resemble the mainstream rivals it rebelled against in its youth: carriers that were slow-growing, complex, and costly to run." Some analysts also raised concerns that the airline would soon start charging for baggage. Despite the setbacks, Southwest posted record annual profits in 2013.

The following year, the company unveiled an updated look by replacing its classic orange color with yellow. As of 2015, Southwest's 46,000-plus employees served more than 90 countries in the U.S. and several other countries. The airline owned approximately 665 jets and made more than 3,400 flights each day.

From its troubled beginnings as a small inter-Texas airline, Southwest has become a legendary success story by putting people first and doing things its own way. "There's no doubt Southwest has proven its model is a winner," said business writer Seth Stevenson. "Sometimes the simplest operations are also the smartest." But the growing Southwest will need to work to keep those operations simple and efficient. As the aviation industry evolves, Southwest Airlines will be fighting to make sure LUV comes out on top.

e want our product, and they want it
get bags for free.... We have had trouble
."

, SENIOR VICE PRESIDENT FOR OPERATIONS

FROM SECRETARY TO PRESIDENT

Colleen Barrett never planned on leading an entire company. "I always loved being a secretary," she said. "All I wanted to do was be very good at what I did." But Barrett, who had proven herself invaluable as cofounder Herb Kelleher's practical-thinking counterpart, found plenty of opportunities to rise through the ranks of Southwest. "As long as I was willing to take the initiative, Herb was willing to let me—or anyone else at the firm—basically do anything we wanted," she said. That openness allowed Barrett and other women to excel in what was otherwise a male-dominated industry. Eventually recognized as one of the most influential leaders in the business, Barrett was hailed for her role in creating Southwest's unique culture. She was also praised for her leadership during major world events that reshaped the airline industry. While other airlines saw losses, Southwest remained profitable every year under her watch.

GLOSSARY

bankruptcy the state of having no money or other valuable belongings, such as property, or being unable to repay debts

board of directors a group of people in charge of making decisions for a publicly owned company

brand the name of a product or manufacturer; a brand distinguishes a product from similar products made by other manufacturers

debt money that is owed to a bank or other lender

domestic occurring inside one country; not international

economy the system of producing, distributing, and consuming of goods within a society

executives decision-making leaders of a company, such as the president or chief executive officer (CEO)

investors people who buy shares of companies or other organizations in exchange for ownership in that company or organization

marketing advertising and promoting a product in order to increase sales

profit the amount of money that a business keeps after subtracting expenses from income

quarter one of four three-month intervals that together comprise the financial year

recession a period of decline in the financial stability of a country or society that typically includes a drop in the stock market, an increase in unemployment, and a decline in home sales

regulated controlled or restricted

revenues the money earned by a company; another word for income

sexist an attitude that discriminates based on sex or gender

shareholders people or corporations who own shares of stock (portions of ownership in a corporation)

slogan a short, attention-grabbing phrase used in advertising

stock shared ownership in a company by many people who buy shares, or portions, of stock, hoping the company will make a profit and the stock value will increase

tarmacs paved areas at an airport where aircraft are parked and boarded

union an organization of workers who join together to protect their common interest and to improve the conditions of their employment, including wages and hours

SELECTED BIBLIOGRAPHY

Brooker, Katrina. "The Chairman of the Board Looks Back." *Fortune*, May 28, 2001. http://archive.fortune.com/magazines/fortune/fortune_archive/2001/05/28/303852/index.htm.

Freiberg, Kevin, and Jackie Freiberg. *Nuts!: Southwest Airlines' Crazy Recipe for Business and Personal Success*. Austin, Tex.: Bard, 1996.

Gittell, Jody Hoffer. *The Southwest Airlines Way: Using the Power of Relationships to Achieve High Performance*. New York: McGraw-Hill, 2003.

Gwynne, S. C. "Mother Nurture." *Texas Monthly*, February 2003. http://www.texasmonthly.com/content/mother-nurture.

Schlesinger, Jennifer. "Ten Minutes that Changed Southwest Airlines' Future." *CNBC*, July 15, 2011. http://www.cnbc.com/id/43768488.

Southwest Airlines Co. "Our History." http://www.swamedia.com/channels/By-Date/pages/history-by-date.

Stevenson, Seth. "The Southwest Secret." *Slate*, June 12, 2012. http://www.slate.com/articles/business/operations/2012/06/southwest_airlines_profitability_how_the_company_uses_operations_theory_to_fuel_its_success_.html.

Note: Every effort has been made to ensure that any websites listed above were active at the time of publication. However, because of the nature of the Internet, it is impossible to guarantee that these sites will remain active indefinitely or that their contents will not be altered.

INDEX